GREAT AND CURIOUS CATS

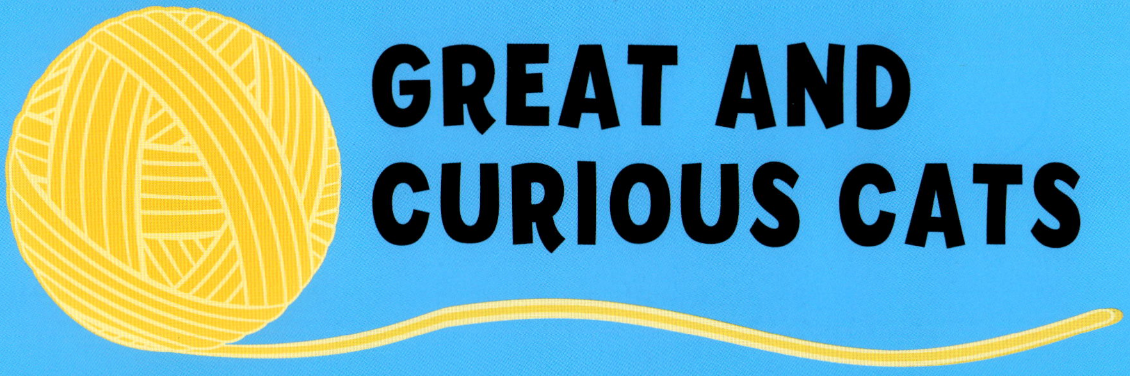

Written by Eliza Jeffery   Illustrated by Marina Halak

Copyright © 2024 Hungry Tomato Ltd

First published in 2024 by Hungry Tomato Ltd
F15, Old Bakery Studios, Blewetts Wharf, Malpas Road, Truro, Cornwall,
TR1 1QH, UK.

No part of this publication may be reproduced, stored in a retrieval system, or transmitted in any form or by any means, electronic, mechanical, photocopying, recording, or otherwise, without prior written permission of the copyright owner.

A CIP catalogue record for this book is available from the British Library.

ISBN 9781835693452

Printed in China

Discover more at
www.hungrytomato.com

CONTENTS

The World of Cats	4
Exercise and Play	6
Cool Cat Features	8
Great and Curious Cats	10
Big and Small	11
Crazy Coats	12
Stunning Eyes	14
One of a Kind	16
Terrific Tails	18
Strange Ears	20
Fun Cat Facts	22
Indoor or Outdoor Cats	24
Name That Cat	26
What's That Cat?	28
Glossary	30
Index	31

Words in **BOLD** can be found in the glossary.

THE WORLD OF CATS

Get ready to explore the wonderful world of cats! From the large Maine coon to the little Singapura, there are so many different types of curious cats to discover.

WHAT IS A SPECIES?

A species is a group of living things, like animals or plants, that share **unique** characteristics. For example, tigers and **domestic** cats are two different species. There are around 40 cat species in total, some of which can be separated into smaller groups called breeds.

Big or small, they've got it all!

WHAT IS A BREED?

A breed is a small group of animals within a species that all share the same (or very similar) appearance and characteristics, making them easy to identify. There are lots of different breeds, and they can vary wildly in size, shape, hairiness, and personality.

Not all cats belong to a specific breed. Some cats are a mixture of lots of different breeds. They can make fantastic and unique pets, and can often be found looking for a loving home at rescue or **rehoming shelters.**

This breed looks very wild, but it is actually a domesticated breed!

WHERE DO CATS COME FROM?

All cats are **descendants** of the African wildcat, a species believed to have appeared 12 million years ago! This cat is still around today, alongside many other types of wild cat. There are plenty of new species that have been domesticated by humans too – these are the types of cats that we keep as pets!

GETTING A CAT?

Maybe you already have a cat in your family, or maybe you'd like to in the future. Owning a cat can be fun and rewarding, but it's also a big responsibility. Some cats need a lot of grooming, care and attention. Before buying or adopting a cat, you should always carefully research their breed and think about whether you are able to give them everything they need to be happy.

Some cats require more care than others!

EXERCISE AND PLAY

When it comes to taking care of a cat, there is a lot to consider! Some cats need a lot more looking after than others. Here are a few things to think about when you're looking into what your cat needs to be happy and healthy.

PLAYTIME

Regardless of whether your cat lives indoors or is allowed to explore the world outside, exercise is important for keeping your cat happy. And the best way for your pet to exercise is through play!

You might want to get involved with playtime, too! This is the perfect way to bond with your cat and make sure it is staying active. Exercise and play are very important in keeping your cat happy, as well as healthy!

A ball of string will keep a cat entertained for ages!

EVERYDAY EXERCISE

Although different cats require slightly different levels of fitness, it is recommended that 30 minutes a day of exercise is a good amount of time for a cat to stay healthy. Unlike dogs, cats don't need long and energetic walks.

Cats that are allowed outdoors will spend lots of their time on the move, but short play sessions at home throughout the day are a great way to keep them happy too. Old cats and cats with health problems will only need short bursts of exercise.

Indoor cats need plenty of exercise, too!

Cats love scratching posts, climbing, and playing with toys.

WALKING AN INDOOR CAT

If you have an indoor cat (see page 22), you can make sure they stay healthy and get enough exercise by walking them on a lead too. It may take your cat some getting used to, but it is a great opportunity for your indoor cat to explore, as well as keep fit.

COOL CAT FEATURES

Explore the unique features that make cats such fascinating creatures! From their sharp claws to their clever tails, uncover the impressive adaptations that help cats thrive in their environments.

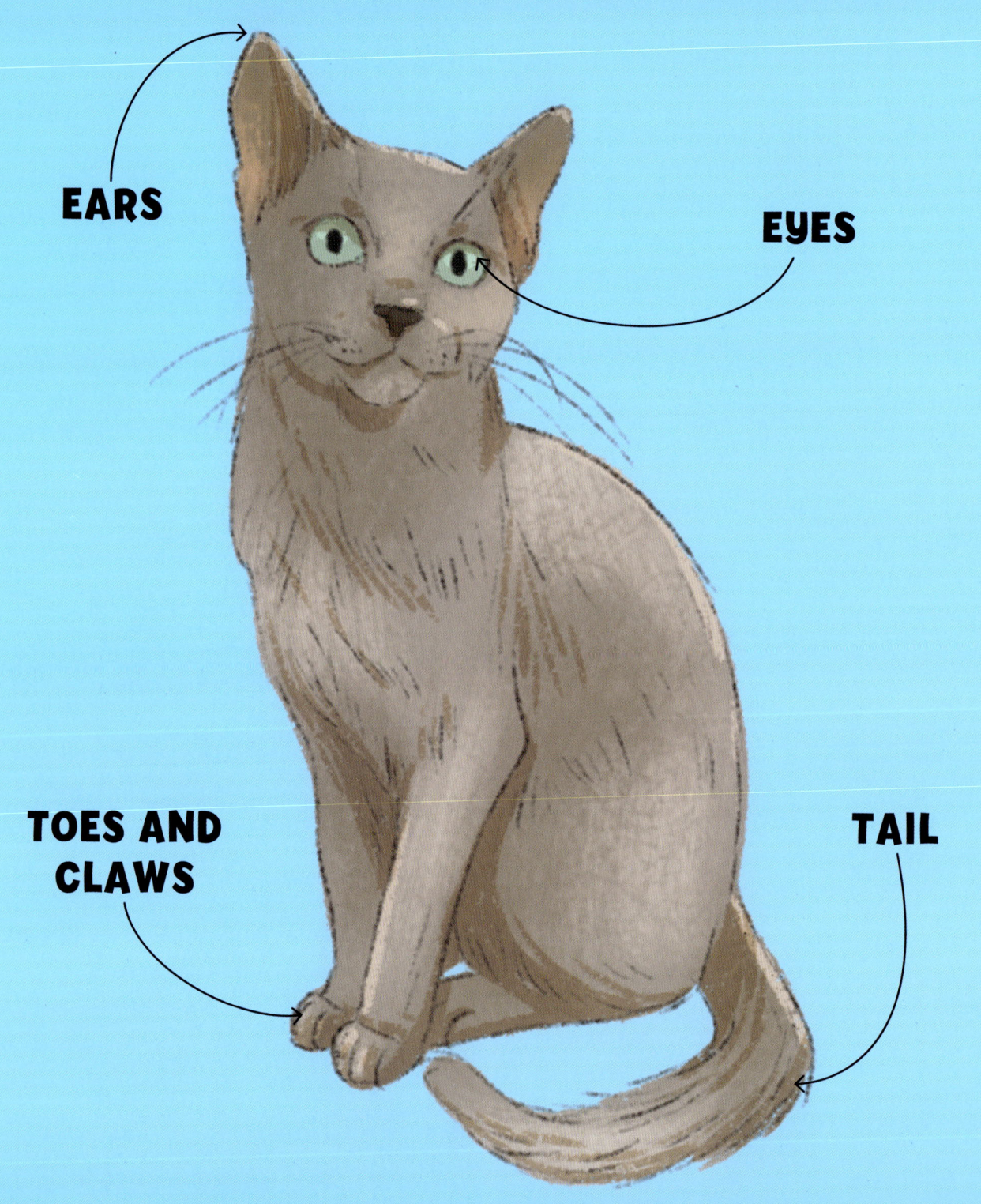

EARS

EYES

TOES AND CLAWS

TAIL

EARS

Cats are able to move each ear independently! This means one ear can be pointing out one way, listening for sounds, while the other can be pointing in the opposite direction.

EYES

Cats have excellent eyesight. Cats can see eight times better than humans can in the dark! They also have an extra eyelid on each eye that protects them from harm, which can't usually be seen.

TOES AND CLAWS

Cats are digitigrade, which means they can walk on their toes! Each toe has a curved claw, which can retract back into the skin.

TAIL

Cats use their tails to help them balance. They have lots of muscles in their tails, which help them move easily and in lots of different ways. Cats also use their tails to show how they are feeling.

GREAT AND CURIOUS CATS

Ever wondered how big the biggest cat really is? Or what a cat with no tail might look like? How about a cat with extremely short legs?

From cats with curly coats to felines without a matching pair of eyes, these quirky and charming characteristics make these one-of-a-kind cats stand out from the crowd. Let's check out the cats with cool and peculiar features!

BIG AND SMALL

Maine Coon

The Maine coon is the largest domestic cat breed in the world. This impressive feline is celebrated as the native cat of America. They have a thick, waterproof coat that thickens in colder months and sheds in warmer months. They can be as big as a medium-sized dog!

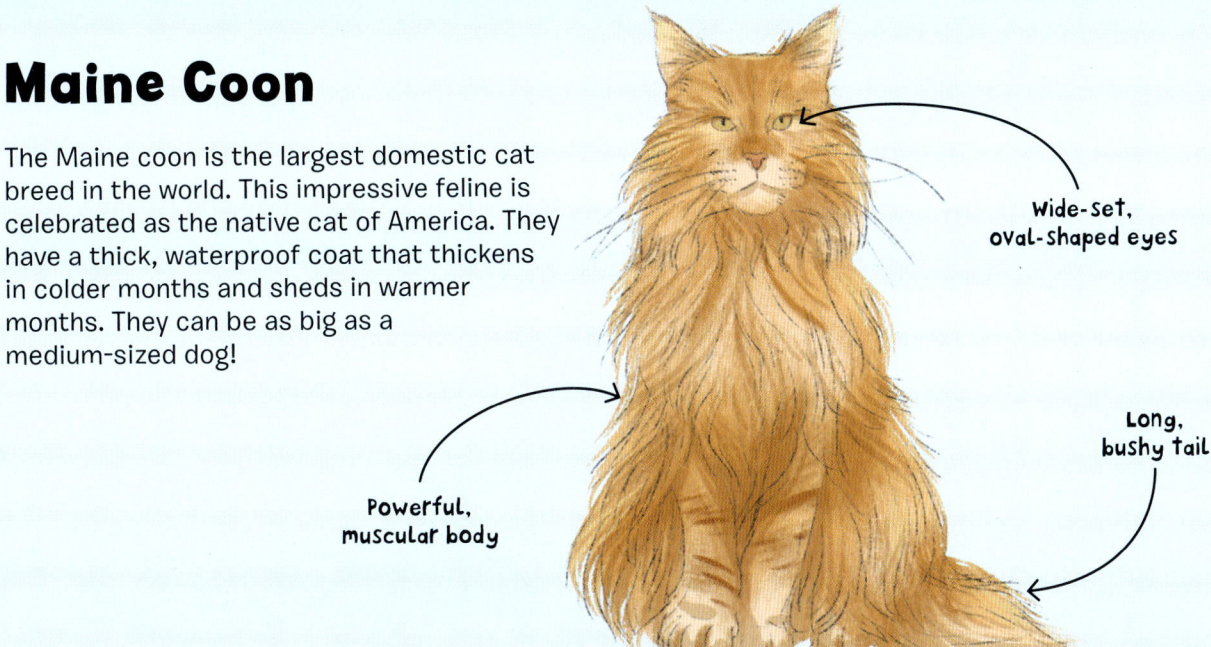

- Wide-set, oval-shaped eyes
- Long, bushy tail
- Powerful, muscular body

ORIGIN: USA
COAT: Silky and smooth
PERSONALITY: Friendly and gentle

GROOMING	🐾	🐾	🐾	·	·
AFFECTION	🐾	🐾	🐾	🐾	·
PLAYFULNESS	🐾	🐾	🐾	🐾	·

Singapura

The Singapura is the smallest cat breed in the world. Despite being small in size, these energetic felines make up for it with their big personalities! They can be very mischievous, and love to explore the world around them.

- Tall, wide ears
- Long, slender bodies
- Large, bulging eyes

ORIGIN: United Kingdom
COAT: Short and smooth
PERSONALITY: Intelligent and curious

GROOMING	🐾	🐾	·	·	·
AFFECTION	🐾	🐾	🐾	🐾	🐾
PLAYFULNESS	🐾	🐾	🐾	🐾	·

GREAT AND CURIOUS CATS

American Wirehair

The American wirehair is best known for its unusual **wiry** coat! The **crimped** fur curls round on itself, making its coat bristly and rough to touch. These cats enjoy playing with their owners but much prefer a quieter indoor space.

- distinctive markings on head
- whiskers can be curly too!
- strong legs for pouncing

ORIGIN: USA
COAT: Wiry and coarse
PERSONALITY: Friendly and active

GROOMING
AFFECTION
PLAYFULNESS

Ural Rex

The Ural Rex has a curly coat too! This is a popular breed for families, due to its patient and playful nature. Gentle, but confident, the Ural Rex will make friends with anybody that it can, including other household pets (even dogs!).

- Large, rounded ears
- Bright, oval-shaped eyes
- Short, soft, curly coat
- Loves to play all day long!

ORIGIN: Russia
COAT: Long and wavy
PERSONALITY: Quiet but friendly

GROOMING
AFFECTION
PLAYFULNESS

CRAZY COATS   13

Sphynx

Sphynx are most well-known for having no fur at all! These hairless felines were named because of how similar they looked to the Egyptian **monument** of the Sphinx. Though their appearance is not appealing to everybody, these cats are very loving and friendly.

- Large, broad ears
- High cheekbones
- Wrinkly skin all over!
- High-maintenance breed that needs a lot of care

ORIGIN: Canada	**GROOMING** 🐾🐾🐾🐾🐾
COAT: None!	**AFFECTION** 🐾🐾🐾🐾🐾
PERSONALITY: Energetic and intelligent	**PLAYFULNESS** 🐾🐾🐾🐾🐾

Lykoi

Because of its unusual coat, the Lykoi is often described as looking like a werewolf! This active feline is partially hairless, with thin fur unevenly covering its body. They may look like **feral** creatures, but these cats make excellent, playful pets.

- Large, oval-shaped eyes
- Hairless whisker pads
- Slender body

ORIGIN: USA	**GROOMING** 🐾🐾🐾🐾🐾
COAT: Uneven and soft	**AFFECTION** 🐾🐾🐾🐾🐾
PERSONALITY: Outgoing and vocal	**PLAYFULNESS** 🐾🐾🐾🐾🐾

GREAT AND CURIOUS CATS

Khao Manee

Khao Manees can have blue, yellow or green eyes and sometimes they don't have a matching pair! They are very talkative and will purr or chirp loudly when they are happy. These fascinating felines are loyal to their owners and do not like to be away from them for too long!

- Pink nose
- Muscular body
- Beautiful white coat!

ORIGIN: Thailand
COAT: Short and smooth
PERSONALITY: Active and people-loving

GROOMING 🐾🐾🐾🐾🐾
AFFECTION 🐾🐾🐾🐾🐾
PLAYFULNESS 🐾🐾🐾🐾🐾

Ojos Azules

Ojos Azules is considered an extremely rare breed. But the distinctive feature that makes this feline stand out is its unusually bright blue eyes! Its breed name even means 'blue eyes' in Spanish.

- Sweet facial expressions
- Small, pink nose
- Likes lots of love and attention!

ORIGIN: USA
COAT: Short and fine
PERSONALITY: Friendly and gentle

GROOMING 🐾🐾🐾🐾🐾
AFFECTION 🐾🐾🐾🐾🐾
PLAYFULNESS 🐾🐾🐾🐾🐾

STUNNING EYES 15

Russian Blue

Russian blue cats are easy to spot, as they have beautiful, bluish coats and piercing, green eyes. It takes roughly four months for these felines to develop these bright eyes, sometimes starting off as shades of amber or yellow.

Bright, round eyes

Soft double coat

Long, thin body

ORIGIN: Russia	
COAT: Thick and dense	
PERSONALITY: Calm and shy	

GROOMING 🐾🐾🐾 🐾 🐾
AFFECTION 🐾🐾🐾 🐾 🐾
PLAYFULNESS 🐾🐾🐾 🐾 🐾

Tall ears with rounded tips

Super climbers and explorers!

GREAT AND CURIOUS CATS

Siamese

One of the most well-known cat breeds in the world is the Siamese. These elegant felines need lots of playtime, especially outdoors. As well as enjoying calm environments, these curious cats love to climb and explore!

Piercing almond-shaped eyes

Darker fur markings on face, ears, paws and tail

Look how high it can climb!

ORIGIN: Thailand
COAT: Fine and short
PERSONALITY: Sociable and athletic

GROOMING 🐾🐾🐾
AFFECTION 🐾🐾🐾🐾
PLAYFULNESS 🐾🐾🐾🐾🐾

Munchkin

Munchkins have extremely short legs! Despite their small size, these active felines love to play high-energy games with their owners and can run very fast. This unique breed can be either long-haired or short-haired.

Round, golden eyes

Thick, waterproof coat

Tail is the same length as its body!

ORIGIN: USA
COAT: Smooth and thick
PERSONALITY: Loyal and energetic

GROOMING 🐾🐾🐾
AFFECTION 🐾🐾🐾🐾
PLAYFULNESS 🐾🐾🐾🐾🐾

ONE OF A KIND

Chausie

The Chausie was originally believed to have developed from a mix of wildcat and domestic cat, giving it its untamed appearance. This striking feline requires lots of company and attention from its owners, and is known to get along well with dogs!

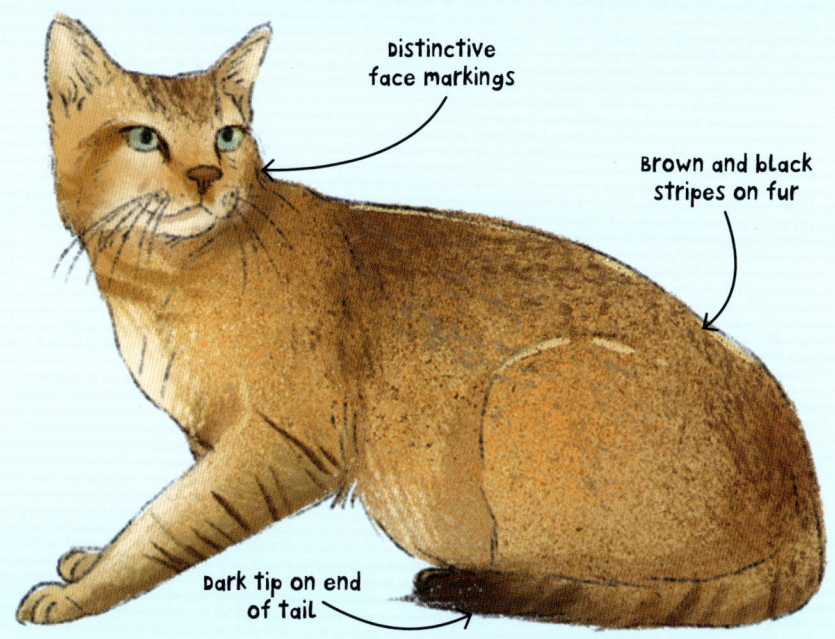

- distinctive face markings
- Brown and black stripes on fur
- Dark tip on end of tail

ORIGIN: USA
COAT: Short and silky
PERSONALITY: Active and curious

GROOMING
AFFECTION
PLAYFULNESS

Egyptian Mau

The Egyptian Mau is one of the only domesticated cats that has a naturally spotted coat. This majestic breed dates back to ancient Egypt, and can be seen in many **tomb** paintings from the time. Although they can be very loving toward their owners, they're very shy and cautious around anybody else!

- Bright, green eyes
- Back legs are longer than front legs!

ORIGIN: Egypt
COAT: Short and dense
PERSONALITY: Friendly and loyal

GROOMING
AFFECTION
PLAYFULNESS

18   GREAT AND CURIOUS CATS

Japanese Bobtail

The Japanese bobtail is easy to spot because of its small, round tail that looks just like the tail of a rabbit. This breed originated in Japan and is believed to bring good luck. This sweet feline would be happy playing with its owners all day long!

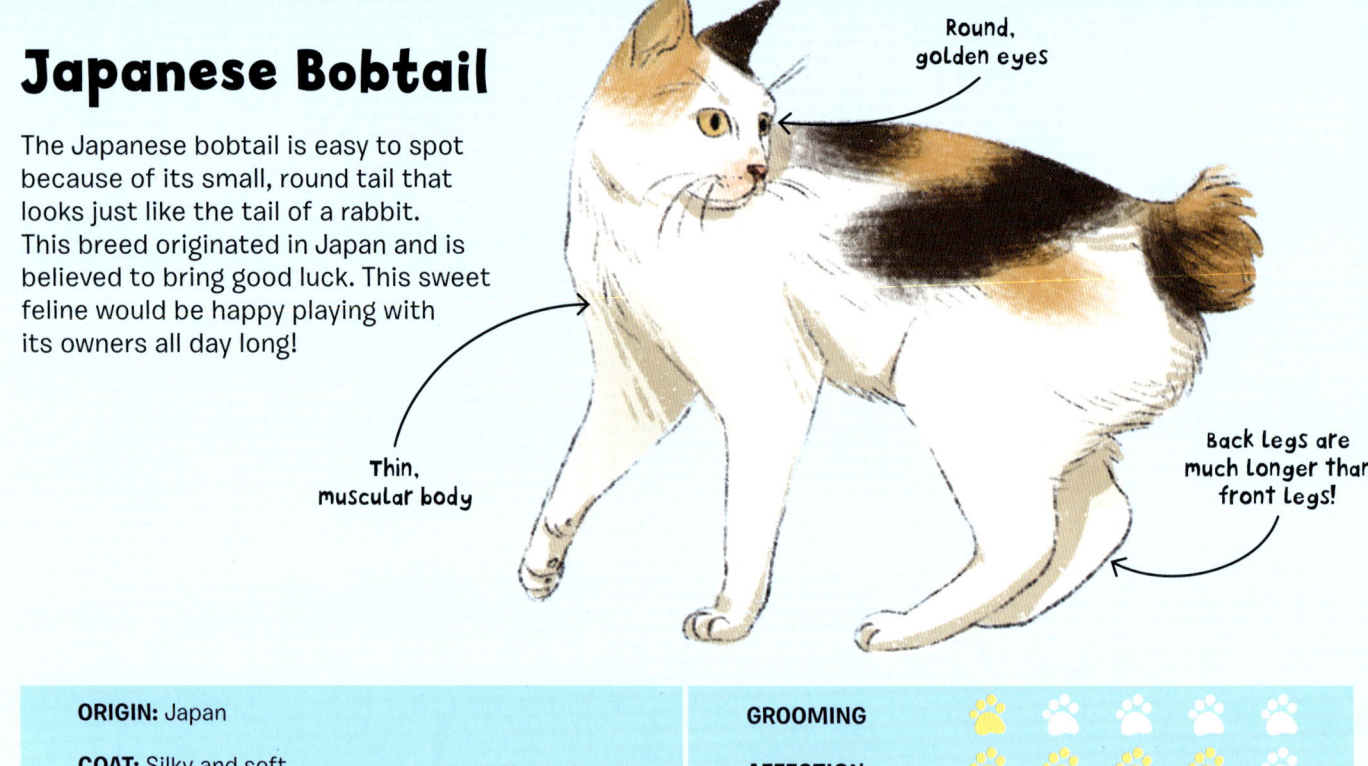

Round, golden eyes

Thin, muscular body

Back legs are much longer than front legs!

ORIGIN: Japan
COAT: Silky and soft
PERSONALITY: Intelligent and outgoing

GROOMING ●○○○○
AFFECTION ●●●●●
PLAYFULNESS ●●●●●

American Ringtail

Like its name suggests, the American ringtail is easily spotted by its tail that is twisted into the shape of a ring. This unique-looking feline is the only cat breed to have a tail like this. They are curious cats, with a particular love for climbing.

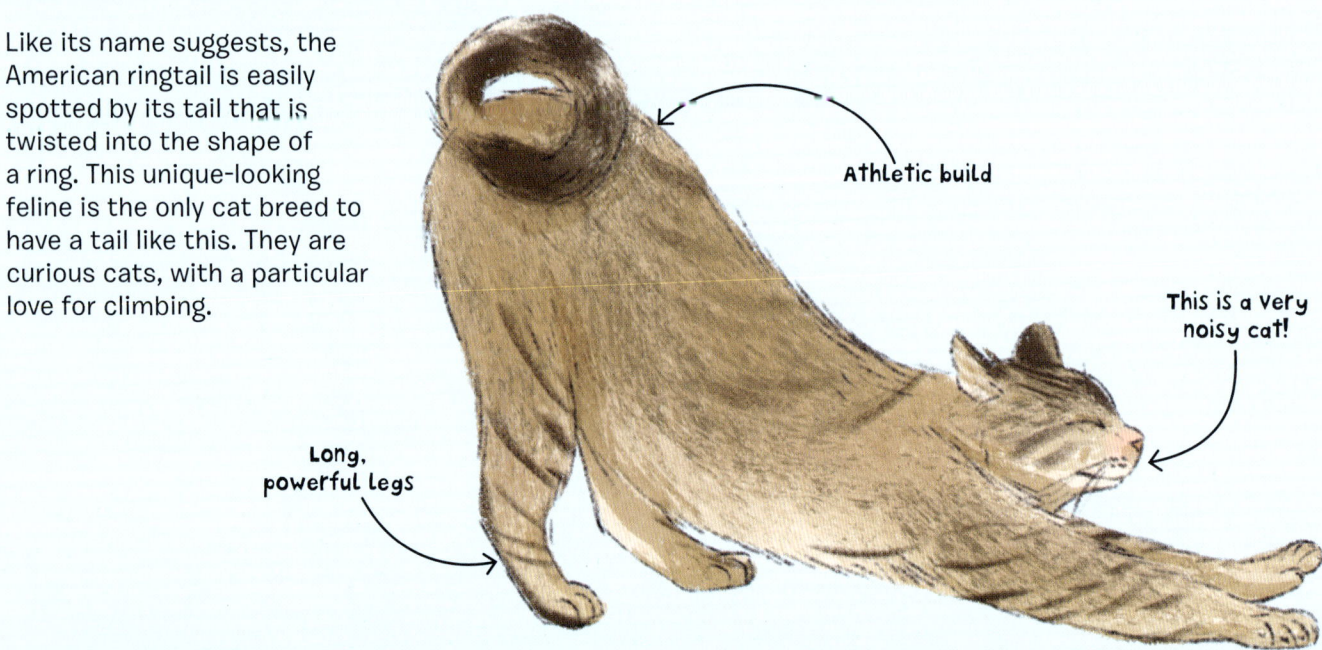

Athletic build

This is a very noisy cat!

Long, powerful legs

ORIGIN: USA
COAT: Silky and soft
PERSONALITY: Active and vocal

GROOMING ●○●○○
AFFECTION ●●●●●
PLAYFULNESS ●●●●○

TERRIFIC TAILS 19

Pixiebob

The Pixiebob gets its name from its extremely short tail. Despite looking like its wildcat relative, the bobcat, this feline is known for its sweet, gentle nature and love of being around people. They are also described as having dog-like personalities because they enjoy playing in water!

sturdy, well-muscled body

Small, red nose

Large, broad paws

ORIGIN: USA
COAT: Woolly and dense
PERSONALITY: Intelligent and sociable

GROOMING
AFFECTION
PLAYFULNESS

Manx

Manx cats have no tail at all! Instead, the end of their small bodies have a short stump where the tail should be. This unusual breed is popular with cat owners for its unique appearance and sweet nature. They are very curious cats, playing with anything they find!

Double-layered coat

Strong back legs

Round face with big cheeks

ORIGIN: United Kingdom
COAT: Thick and dense
PERSONALITY: Gentle and calm

GROOMING
AFFECTION
PLAYFULNESS

GREAT AND CURIOUS CATS

Scottish Fold

Scottish folds are best known for having large, golden eyes and folded over ears! Their unique ears bend forward and lay flat against their head. These cats are known for being very loyal creatures, and love quality time with their owners.

Sweet facial expressions

Short neck

Rounded, solid body

ORIGIN: Scotland
COAT: Short and dense
PERSONALITY: Quiet and friendly

GROOMING
AFFECTION
PLAYFULNESS

American Curl

Similar to the Highlander (page 21), the American curl, as its name suggests, has ears that curl far back on the top of its head. Sociable and nosy, American curls love to be involved in their owners' lives, 'helping' them as much as possible!

Distinctive, striped markings on fur

Thick, bushy tail

Rectangular-shaped body

ORIGIN: USA
COAT: Soft and silky
PERSONALITY: Loving and engaging

GROOMING
AFFECTION
PLAYFULNESS

STRANGE EARS 21

Highlander

The Highlander is a fairly new breed of cat and is best known for ears that bend backward. These energetic cats are always in the mood to play! They are loyal to their owners, and can be either short-haired or long-haired.

Stripy or spotty fur, and sometimes has both!

Well-built, strong body

Large, round paws

ORIGIN: USA
COAT: Soft and thick
PERSONALITY: Active and loving

GROOMING
AFFECTION
PLAYFULNESS

Can play all day long

Has a short tail that wags when it's happy!

FUN CAT FACTS

What else is there to know about the wonderful world of cats? Let's uncover more interesting facts about these fascinating felines.

AFFECTIONATE CATS

Cats lick their owners to show they care! A cat associates licking with caring as it is something they learn from their mothers, who lick their kittens from birth. As they grow, kittens carry on sharing the love with those around them, whether they are cats or humans!

Your cat's tongue may be rough, but its a sign of love!

AND JUMP!

Cats of all kinds are known for their agility. On average, a cat can jump up to six times their height in one jump! How impressive is that?

LANDING FEET FIRST

As well as jumping up high, cats are impressive when they land back down too! All cats are born with the 'righting reflex', a system which allows them to move in mid-air so they land paws first.

WHISKERS ALL OVER

Cats don't just have whiskers on their face! All cats have carpal whiskers too, which are special whiskers found on their front legs, just above their paws. The carpal whiskers help cats climb trees, as well as help them navigate their environment.

INDOOR OR OUTDOOR CATS

An important decision to make when getting a feline friend is whether they will be an indoor or outdoor cat. While both options have their benefits and risks, it's important to think about what's best for your own cat's safety, health, and overall happiness.

INDOOR CATS

Some cats prefer not go outside on their own, but may explore the outside world with their owner. There are positives to keeping your cat indoors, such as protecting them from outdoor dangers, like cars and predators.

However, indoor cats may sometimes feel restless, so they need plenty of toys and activities to keep them entertained. They may also become more nervous compared to outdoor cats, who are used to the sights and sounds of the outside world.

It's important for indoor cats to have plenty of physical exercise, attention, and play to keep them happy and healthy.

American wirehair cats are indoor cats as they prefer the comfort of their home.

OUTDOOR CATS

Outdoor cats are cats that are allowed to explore the outside world without their owner. Going outdoors can be enjoyable for your cat as it gives them the freedom and space to explore, as well as to hunt.

Singapura cats are very curious, playful, and like the outdoors!

However, outdoor cats face risks such as the possibility of injury from fights with other animals or getting sick from **diseases**. **Parasites** like fleas and ticks are something that owners will have to regularly check their cat's fur for.

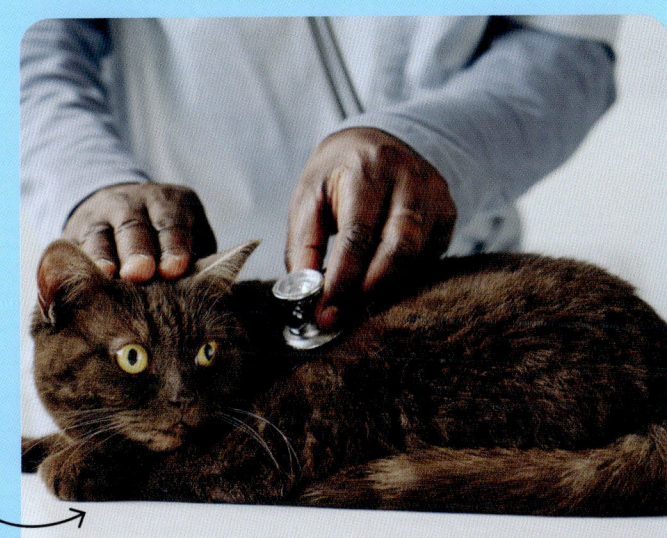

It's also important that outdoor cats are given the necessary medicine and care to keep them safe and healthy.

Outdoor cats sometimes bring **rodents** they've hunted and caught back to the house! Although we might not be too happy about it, cats often bring back their **prey** as a gift for their owners!

NAME THAT CAT

Can you work out which cat each of these pictures are a part of? Clues have been provided for you based on facts in this book.

CLUE: These cats are believed to be a mix of wildcat and domestic cat.

CLUE: These cats look a bit like werewolves due to their unusual, partially hairless coat.

CLUE: These cats are the largest domestic breed in the world!

CLUE: These cats are named after their bright blue eyes!

CLUE: These cats are easy to spot due to their small, round tail that looks like the tail of a rabbit.

CLUE: These cats are known for having large, golden eyes and folded over ears that lay flat against their heads.

CLUE: These cats have a tail that is twisted into the shape of a ring.

CLUE: These cats have extremely short legs.

CLUE: These cats are the smallest cat breed in the world!

CLUE: These cats are well-known for having no fur at all! They look similar to the Egyptian monument of the Sphinx.

Answers can be found on page 32.

WHAT'S THAT CAT?

Now that you have read all about these curious cats, how good are you at identifying them? There are 20 different cats to figure out. Use the information in the book to help you.

1. What am I?
A. Maine Coon
B. Singapura
C. Chausie

2. What am I?
A. Khao Manee
B. Singapura
C. Munchkin

3. What am I?
A. Manx
B. American Curl
C. Ojos Azules

4. What am I?
A. Siamese
B. Scottish Fold
C. Ural Rex

5. What am I?
A. Sphynx
B. Highlander
C. Manx

6. What am I?
A. Russian Blue
B. Sphynx
C. Siamese

7. What am I?
A. Lykoi
B. Japanese Bobtail
C. Munchkin

8. What am I?
A. Egyptain Mau
B. Ojos Azules
C. Munchkin

9. What am I?
A. Ural Rex
B. Khao Manee
C. Russian Blue

10. What am I?
A. American Ringtail
B. Egyptian Mau
C. Pixiebob

Answers can be found on page 32.

What am I?
A. Chausie
B. American Wirehair
C. Manx

What am I?
A. Highlander
B. American Curl
C. Russian Blue

What am I?
A. Siamese
B. Japanese Bobtail
C. Scottish Fold

What am I?
A. Ojos Azules
B. Ural Rex
C. American Ringtail

What am I?
A. Lykoi
B. American Wirehair
C. Highlander

What am I?
A. Sphynx
B. Pixiebob
C. Scottish Fold

What am I?
A. Scottish Fold
B. Lykoi
C. Khao Manee

What am I?
A. Maine Coon
B. Pixiebob
C. Singapura

What am I?
A. American Wirehair
B. Maine Coon
C. Egyptian Mau

What am I?
A. American Curl
B. Chausie
C. Siamese

GLOSSARY

Crimped - fur that has small ridges or folds in it.

Descendants - people or animals that are related to an individual or group who lived in the past. For example, you are a descendant of your parents and grandparents.

Diseases - conditions that cause part of a living thing to no longer work properly.

Domestic - an animal that has been tamed or trained to live or work with humans.

Environments - another word for surroundings.

Feral - wild, not domestic (see above).

Monument - a statue or building made in memory of a person or event.

Parasites - tiny creatures that live on or inside other living things, like animals or plants.

Prey - animals that are hunted and killed for food.

Rehoming shelter - a place where cats (or other animals) who were lost, stray or given up by their owners are looked after until they can be adopted into a new home.

Retract - to pull something back or make it go back inside.

Rodents - small mammals with sharp front teeth, such as mice or squirrels.

Slender - something that is thin and narrow.

Tomb - a large, underground space for burying and remembering the dead.

Unique - something that stands out and is completely different from everything else.

Wiry - a type of coat that is rough, thick and bristly.

INDEX

A
agility 22
American curl 20, 28-29, 32
American ringtail 18, 28-29, 32
American wirehair 12, 24, 28-29, 32

C
Chausie 17, 28-29, 32

E
Egyptian Mau 17, 28-29, 32
exercise 6-7, 24

F
features 8-9
    ears 8-9, 11, 12-13, 15, 16
       20-21, 22, 27
    eyes 8-9, 11, 12-13, 14-15,
       16-17, 18, 20, 22, 26
    tails 8-9, 11, 16-17, 18-19,
       20-21, 22, 27
    whiskers 12-13, 23, 27

H
Highlander 20-21, 28-29, 32

I
indoor cats 7, 24-25

J
Japanese bobtail 18, 28-29, 32

K
Khao Manee 14, 28-29, 32

L
Lykoi 13, 28-29, 32

M
Maine coon 4, 11, 23, 28-29, 32
Manx 19, 28-29, 32
Munchkin 16, 28-29, 32

O
Ojos Azules 14, 28-29, 32
outdoor cats 24-25

P
Pixiebob 19, 28-29, 32
playtime 6-7, 16

R
Russian Blue 15, 28-29, 32

S
Scottish fold 20, 28-29, 32
Siamese 16, 28-29, 32
Singapura 4, 11, 23, 25, 28-29, 32
species 4-5
Sphynx 13, 28-29, 32

U
Ural Rex 12, 28-29, 32

NAME THAT CAT ANSWERS

1 - Chausie
2 - Lykoi
3 - Maine Coon
4 - Ojos Azules
5 - Japanese Bobtail
6 - Scottish Fold
7 - American Ringtail
8 - Munchkin
9 - Singapura
10 - Sphynx

WHAT'S THAT CAT ANSWERS

1 - A. Maine Coon
2 - B. Singapura
3 - A. Manx
4 - C. Ural Rex
5 - A. Sphynx
6 - C. Siamese
7 - C. Munchkin
8 - B. Ojos Azules
9 - B. Khao Manee
10 - B. Egyptian Mau
11 - A. Chausie
12 - C. Russian Blue
13 - B. Japanese Bobtail
14 - C. American Ringtail
15 - C. Highlander
16 - C. Scottish Fold
17 - B. Lykoi
18 - B. Pixiebob
19 - A. American Wirehair
20 - A. American Curl

Picture Credits:
(abbreviations: t=top, b=bottom, m=middle, l=left, r=right)

8H 28ml; Akifyeva S 28tr; Andrey_Kuzmin 7br; AnnaStills 25mr; AntonMaltsev 24mr; ANURAK PONGIPATIMET 26tl; Azovsky 29bl; Bachkova Natalia 9br; Bal Iryna 28ml; Bamgraphy 28bl; Cicafotos 29mr; COULANGES 29mr, 29tl; DenisNata 9tl; Everydoghasastory 28tr; Fernando Calmon 24bl; Goldeneden 7ml; Irina Brododovskaya 29tl; Iv-olga 28mr; Ivanova N 29ml; Jojosmb 25tl; Konstantin Raskudakin 9tr; Luna Vandoorne 24tl; Magui RF 6m; Nils Jacobi 27br, 27tl; Nynke Van Holten 29tr, 28br; Patrick Hatt 29ml; Rita_Kochmarjova 26br; Romauld Cisakowski 25bl; Seregraff 29br; Svetlana Rey 9bl; Sviatoslav_Shevchenko 28mr; VictorTaurus 28tl; Wirestock Creators 29tr; Seregraff 28tl.

Every effort has been made to trace the copyright holders, and we apologise in advance for any unintentional omissions. We would be pleased to insert the appropriate acknowledgements in any subsequent edition of this publication.

ABOUT THE AUTHOR

Eliza Jeffery is a children's book author based in Falmouth. She is passionate about helping children explore and enjoy the big world around them. She loves exploring Cornwall, and can often be found reading a book and eating a bowl of mussels by the sea!

ABOUT THE ILLUSTRATOR

Marina Halak is a talented illustrator of children's books from Ukraine. Her stunning illustrations are inspired by her own childhood, children, nature, magical moments and fairy tales. Marina is also the illustrator behind the series, *Dogs*.